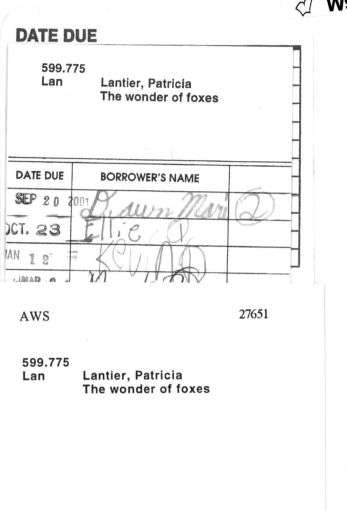

DATE DUE

599.775
Lan   Lantier, Patricia
The wonder of foxes

DATE DUE	BORROWER'S NAME	
SEP 20 2001	Dawn Mari	②
OCT. 23	Ellie	
JAN 12	Kevin	
MAR		

AWS   27651

599.775
Lan   Lantier, Patricia
The wonder of foxes

The Wonder of
FOXES

To Kyle
— Judy Schuler

Please visit our web site at: www.garethstevens.com
For a free color catalog describing Gareth Stevens Publishing's list of high-quality books
and multimedia programs, call 1-800-542-2595 (USA) or 1-800-461-9120 (Canada).
Gareth Stevens Publishing's Fax: (414) 332-3567.

Library of Congress Cataloging-in-Publication Data available upon request from publisher.
Fax: (414) 336-0157 for the attention of the Publishing Records Department.

ISBN 0-8368-2765-1

First published in North America in 2001 by
Gareth Stevens Publishing
A World Almanac Education Group Company
330 West Olive Street, Suite 100
Milwaukee, WI 53212 USA

This edition is based on the book *Foxes for Kids,* text © 1998 by Judy Schuler, with illustrations by
John F. McGee, first published in the United States in 1998 by NorthWord Press, (Creative
Publishing international, Inc.), Minnetonka, MN, and published as *Fox Magic for Kids* in a library
edition by Gareth Stevens, Inc., in 2000. Additional end matter © 2001 by Gareth Stevens, Inc.

Photographs © 1998: Tom Vezo: Cover; Tom & Pat Leeson: 7, 8-9, 10, 31, 32, 42-43; D. Robert
Franz/The Wildlife Collection: 12-13, 46-47; Bill Silliker, Jr.: 15; David A. Brunetti: 16; Henry H.
Holdsworth/Uniphoto: 19; Nora & Rick Bowers: 22; Bill Lea: 25; Alan & Sandy Carey: 26-27, 35, 36,
39; Richard Day/Daybreak Imagery: 40.

Printed in the United States of America

1 2 3 4 5 6 7 8 9 05 04 03 02 01

The Wonder of
FOXES

by Patricia Lantier and Judy Schuler
Illustrations by John F. McGee

Gareth Stevens Publishing
A WORLD ALMANAC EDUCATION GROUP COMPANY

In winter, many animals are busy. Rabbits hop, deer run, and squirrels chatter.

Wait a minute! There is a flash of color in the snow. It's a fox!

Foxes are swift, clever mammals. They are the smallest members of the dog family. In fact, male foxes are called dogs. Female foxes are called vixens. Baby foxes are called pups.

red fox (also on next page)

Foxes rub a special scent on rocks and trees to let other foxes know where they live.

red dog fox

Red foxes are the most common foxes. They live in North America and Europe. There are four other species, or types, of foxes in North America. They are the arctic, kit, swift, and gray foxes.

red fox

Most red foxes are a rusty
orange color, but some can
be yellow-red or silver-black.

A red fox, no matter what
color, has a white tip at the
end of its tail.

Foxes live in dens. A fox den is usually a burrow in the ground. Red foxes often build their dens near water.

red fox pups

Sometimes foxes use the old dens of other animals, such as woodchucks and badgers. A vixen will clean out many unused dens before picking one to move into. The vixen's pups will be born and raised in the den.

a well-hidden fox den

Arctic foxes live on the tundra. Thick fur coats keep them from getting cold.

These thick coats are very warm — even warmer than a polar bear's coat!

Arctic foxes are usually white in winter and brown in summer. Their fluffy tails are the same color as the fur on their bodies.

arctic fox

Kit foxes live in northern Mexico and the southwestern desert areas of the United States. Furry feet and thick body fur protect them from the hot sun and sand. Their fur also keeps them warm on cold desert nights. Kit foxes have black tips at the ends of their long tails.

Swift foxes can be found in the area from northern Texas to southern Canada.

These foxes also have black tips at the ends of their tails. Swift foxes are *fast!* They can run up to 40 miles (64 kilometers) per hour.

swift fox

Gray foxes live in North and South America. They are the only foxes that can climb trees.

gray fox

Scientists say foxes are carnivores, or meat eaters. They are really omnivores, which means they will eat whatever they can find — berries, corn, and even other animals.

red fox pup

Foxes have a good sense of smell that helps them find food and know where other foxes live. Foxes also have good eyesight. Their eyes reflect light, like a mirror, so they can see well in the dark. Foxes are nocturnal animals. They hunt and play at night and sleep during the day.

Fox pups are born in late winter or early spring. A mother fox keeps her litter warm by curling herself around the babies and covering them with her warm, bushy tail. The pups are born toothless and blind. They open their eyes when they are about two weeks old.

red fox pups

The dog fox brings food to
the vixen until the newborn
pups are old enough to stay
alone in the den for a while.

By eating the prey their parents bring them, pups learn which animals to hunt when they grow up.

Pups must learn to watch out for large birds, wildcats, bears, and coyotes. Adult foxes teach their pups how to stay safe from predators. Young foxes are usually on their own by the time they are six months old. By nine months, pups are fully grown.

If a young pup wanders away,
its mother carries it home.
She grabs the fur on the back
of its neck with her mouth.

Foxes even have fur between their toes. This fur and soft toe pads help them walk quietly.

Foxes use many different sounds to talk to each other. Sometimes they whine like dogs. At other times they howl or yap. An adult fox may bark sharply to warn its pups of danger.

red fox pups

Fox pups fight playfully.
Play-fighting helps pups
learn to defend themselves
when they are older.

When foxes have plenty to eat, they sometimes hide extra food by neatly burying it. They save this food and eat it at times when food is scarce.

Foxes in the
wild usually
live to be five
or six years old.
When they are
grown, young
females go off
to look for new
dens where they
can raise pups
of their own.

Young male
foxes leave the
den to look
for their own
territories.

The next time
you are in the
woods, maybe
you will see a
flash of color.
It could be a fox!

Glossary

burrow — a hole or tunnel in the ground that an animal digs for shelter

litter — the young from one birth

mammal — an animal with hair or fur that feeds its young with mother's milk

nocturnal — at rest during the day and active at night

predators — animals that hunt other animals for food

prey — animals that are hunted by other animals for food

scarce — difficult to find

species — a group of animals or plants with similar characteristics

territory — an area of land occupied and defended by an animal

tundra — the flat, treeless land often found in Arctic areas

Index

YGNACIO VALLEY
CHRISTIAN SCHOOL
4977 Concord Boulevard
Concord, California 94521